# Handwriting Practice Cursive

## Children's Reading & Writing Education Books

All Rights reserved. No part of this book may be reproduced or used in any way or form or by any means whether electronic or mechanical, this means that you cannot record or photocopy any material ideas or tips that are provided in this book

Copyright 2016

Trace the cursive
letters and words.


Rewrite the letters and
words in the space provided.

*Aa Aa Aa Aa Aa*

*Aa*

*A*

*a*

*A is for Ant.*

Bb Bb Bb Bb

Bb

B

b

B is for Bear.

Cc Cc Cc Cc Cc

Cc

C

c

C is for Cat.

Dd Dd Dd Dd

Dd

D

d

D is for Dog.

*Ee   Ee   Ee   Ee   Ee*

*Ee*

*E*

*e*

*E is for Elephant.*

*Ff  Ff  Ff  Ff  Ff*

*Ff*

*F*

*f*

*F is for Fox.*

*Gg Gg Gg Gg*

*Gg*

*G*

*g*

*G is for Goat.*

*Hh   Hh   Hh   Hh*

*Hh*

*H*

*h*

*H is for Hawk.*

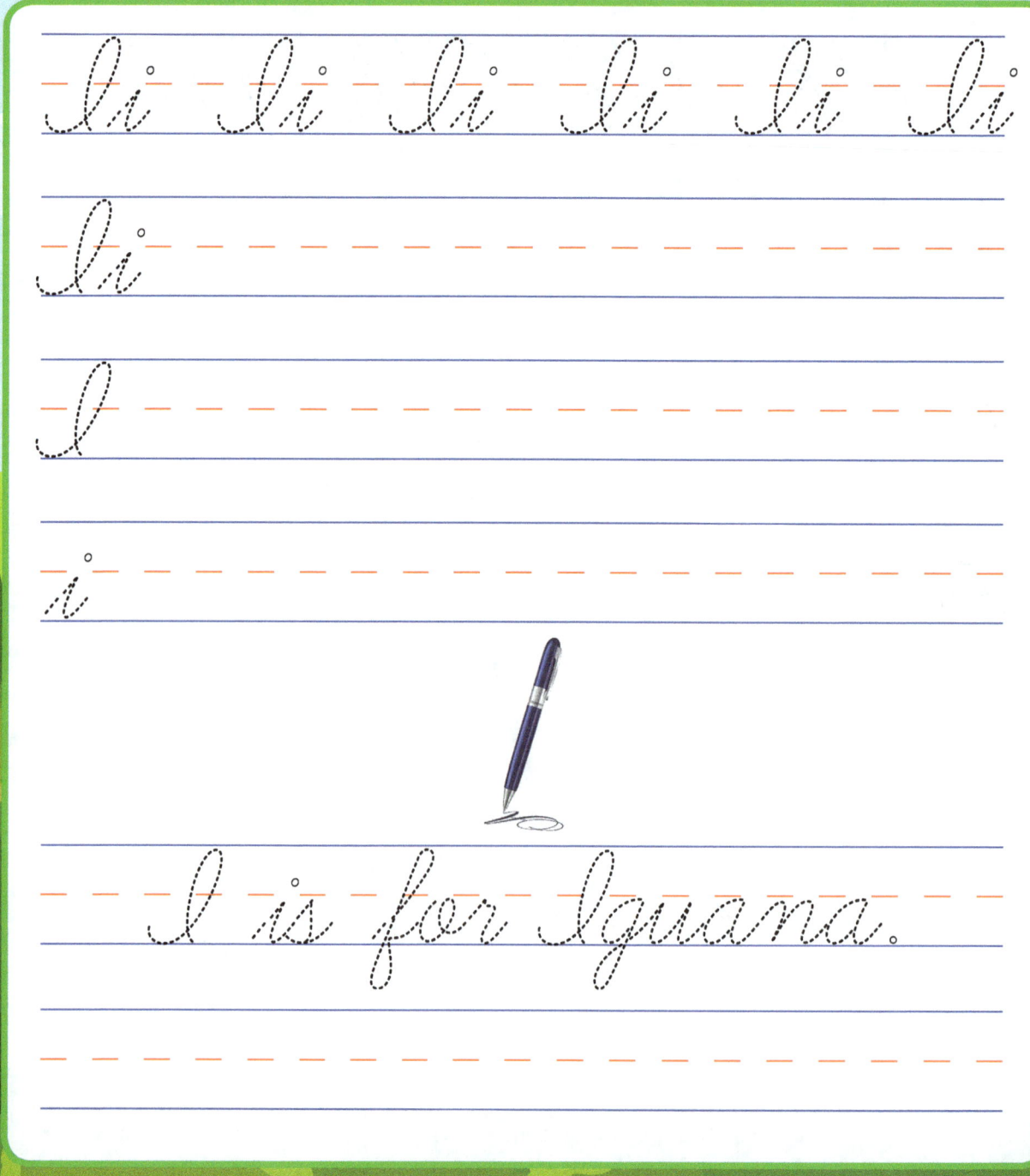

Ii Ii Ii Ii Ii Ii

Ii

I

i

I is for Iguana.

*Jj Jj Jj Jj Jj Jj*

*Jj*

*J*

*j*

J is for Jaguar.

*Kk   Kk   Kk   Kk   Kk*

*Kk*

*K*

*k*

*K is for Kangaroo*

Ll Ll Ll Ll Ll

Ll

L

l

L is for Lion.

*Mm Mm Mm*

*Mm*

*M*

*m*

*M is for Monkey.*

Nn Nn Nn Nn

Nn

N

n

N is for Narwhal.

*Pp Pp Pp Pp Pp*

*Pp*

*P*

*P*

*P is for Penguin.*

*Qq Qq Qq Qq Qq*

*Qq*

*Q*

*q*

*Q is for Quail.*

Rr  Rr  Rr  Rr  Rr

Rr

R

r

R is for Rabbit.

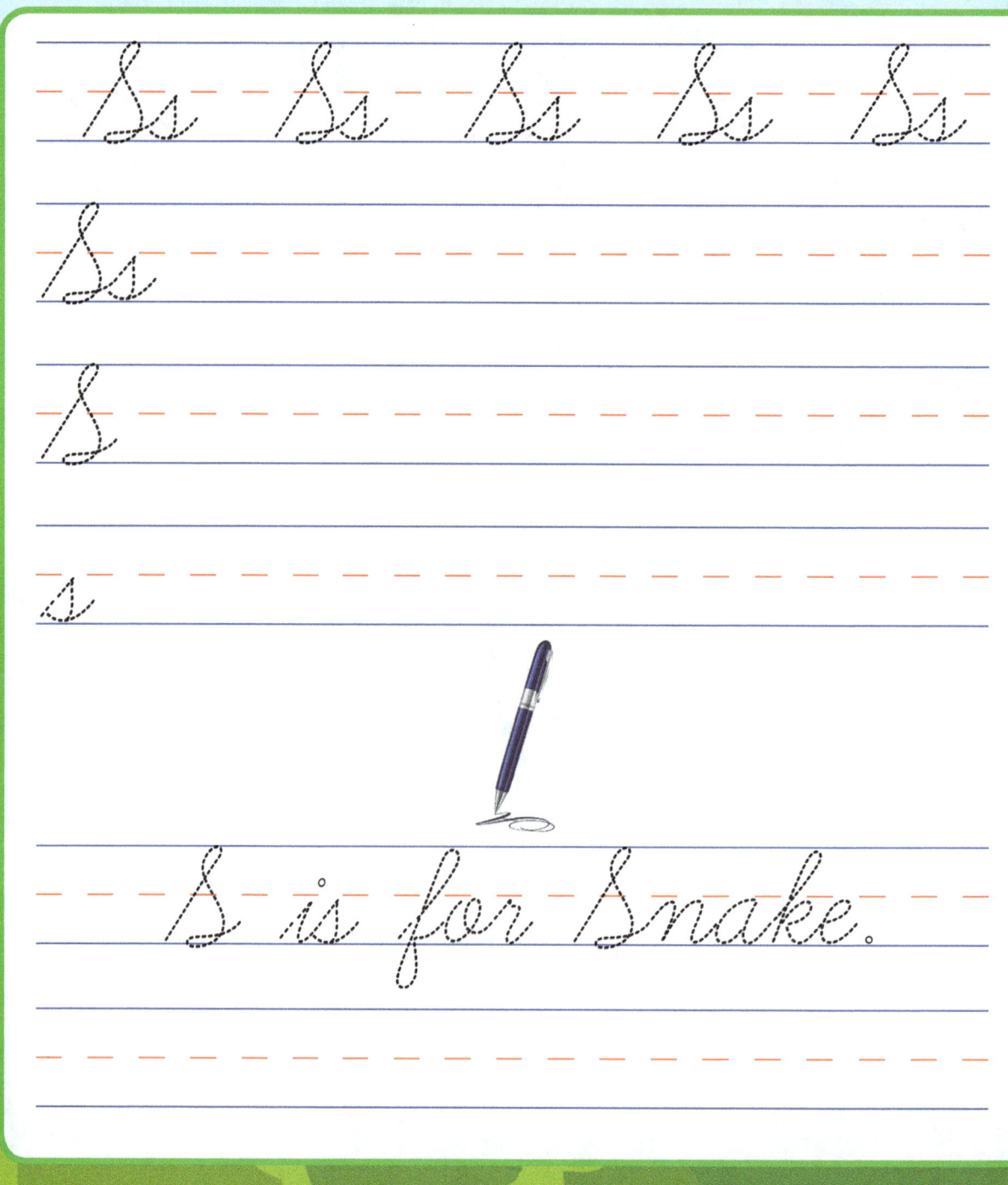

*Tt Tt Tt Tt Tt Tt*

*Tt*

*T*

*t*

*T is for Tiger.*

*Uu Uu Uu Uu*

*Uu*

*U*

*u*

*U is for Uakari.*

*Vv Vv Vv Vv*

*Vv*

*V*

*v*

*V is for Vulture.*

*Ww Ww Ww*

*Ww*

*W*

*w*

*W is for Walrus.*

*Xx   Xx   Xx   Xx*

*Xx*

*X*

*x*

*X is for X-ray fish.*

*Yy Yy Yy Yy Yy*

*Yy*

*Y*

*y*

*Y is for Yak.*

*Zz Zz Zz Zz Zz*

*Zz*

*Z*

*z*

*Z is for Zebra.*

**Trace the cursive sentences and rewrite them in the space provided.**

My dog is eating.

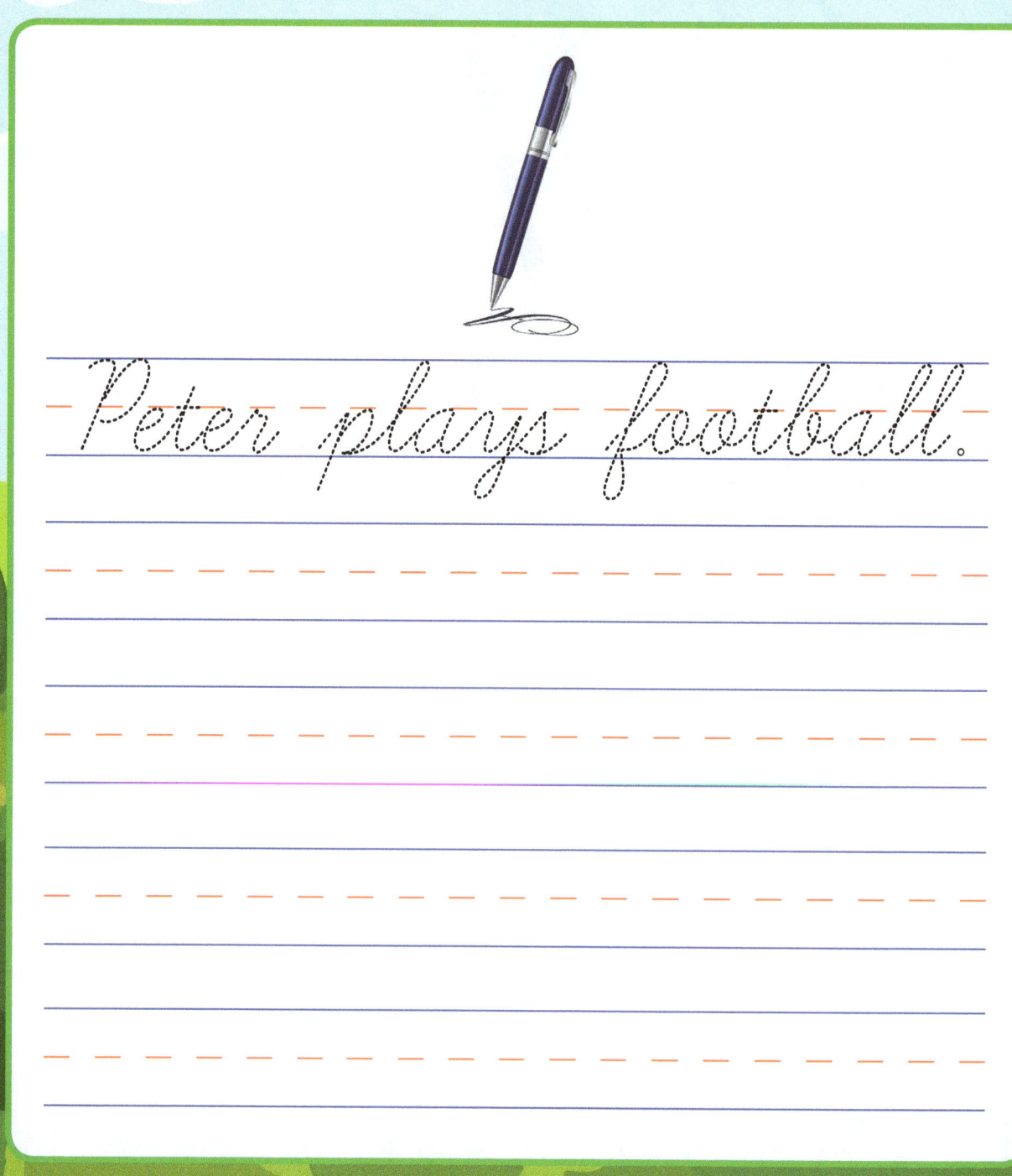

Peter plays football.

*Ben is studying.*

*I love to write.*

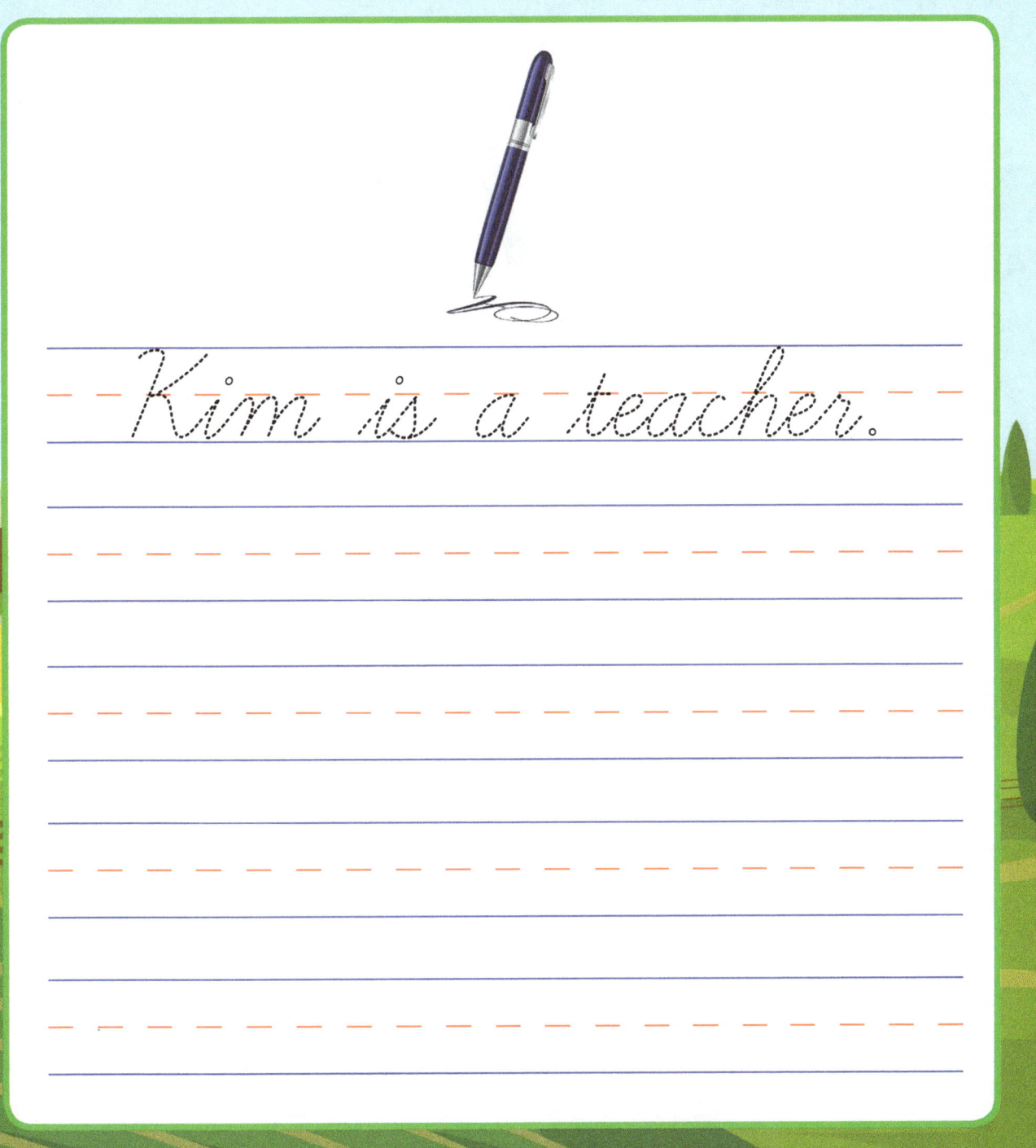

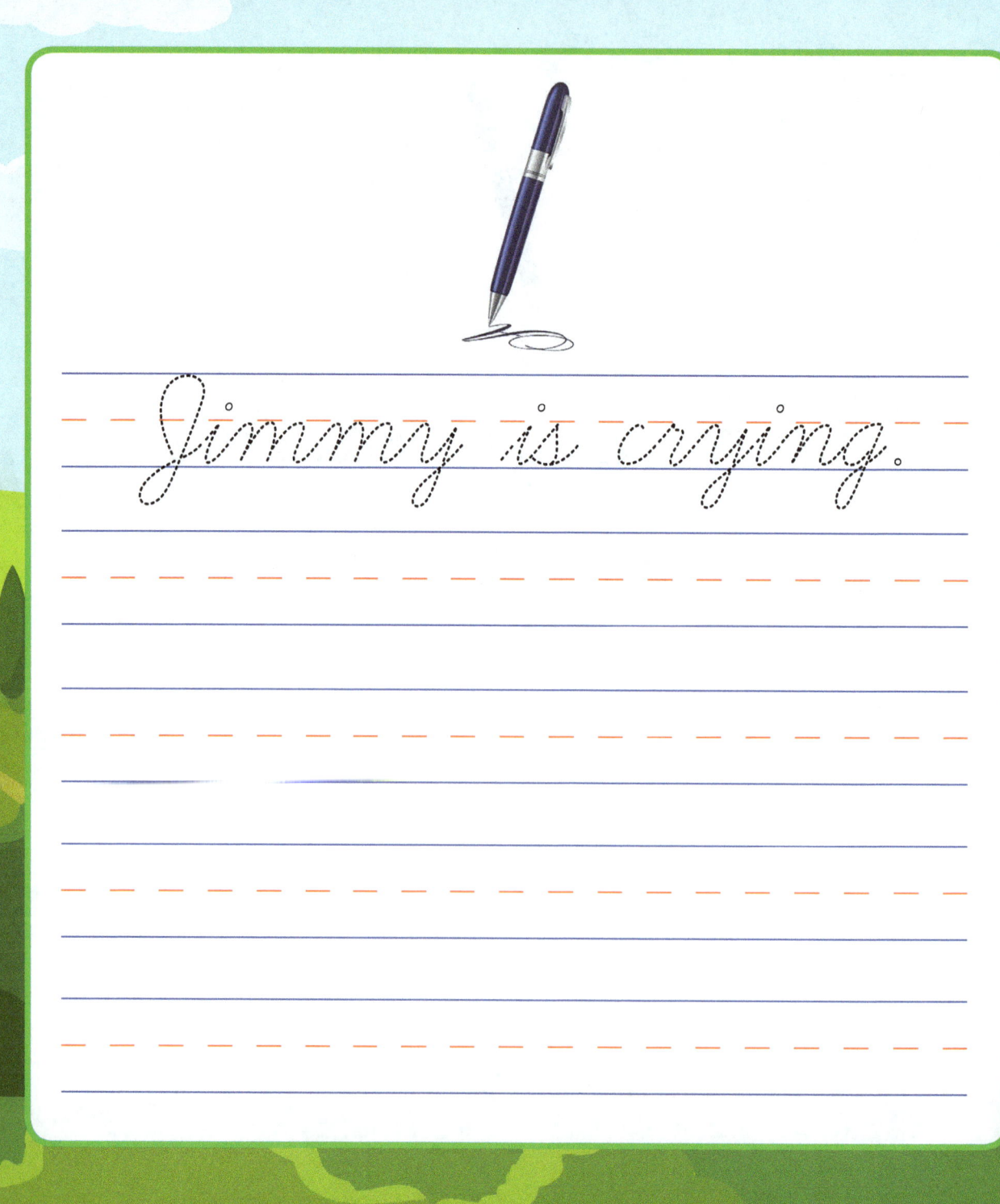

Richell loves dogs.

www.ingramcontent.com/pod-product-compliance
Lightning Source LLC
LaVergne TN
LVHW061323060426
835507LV00019B/2271